A New Tune A Day

Pop Performance Pieces
for Violin

Chord symbols for all pieces are included
for guitar or keyboard accompaniment.

T0078987

Boston Music Company
part of The Music Sales Group
London/New York/Paris/Sydney/Copenhagen/Berlin/Madrid/Hong Kong/Tokyo

Contents

Published by

Boston Music Company

Exclusive Distributors:

Music Sales Limited

14-15 Berners Street, London W1T 3LJ, UK.

Music Sales Corporation

257 Park Avenue South, New York, NY 10010, USA.

Music Sales Pty Limited

20 Resolution Drive, Caringbah, NSW 2229, Australia.

Order No. BM12683

ISBN: 978-1-78038-511-2

Produced by shedwork.com
Photography by Matthew Ward

Printed in the EU

Your Guarantee of Quality

As publishers, we strive to produce every book to the highest commercial standards. The music has been freshly engraved and the book has been carefully designed to minimise awkward page turns and to make playing from it a real pleasure. Throughout, the printing and binding have been planned to ensure a sturdy, attractive publication which should give years of enjoyment. If your copy fails to meet our high standards, please inform us and we will gladly replace it.

www.musicsales.com

American Pie

Words & Music by Don McLean
© Copyright 1971 Mayday Music, USA.
Universal/MCA Music Limited.
All rights in Germany administered by Universal/MCA Music Publ. GmbH.
All Rights Reserved. International Copyright Secured.

Slowly

Moderately

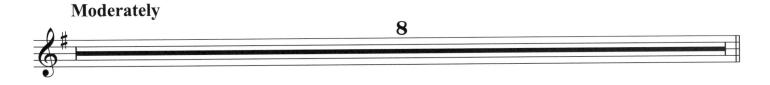

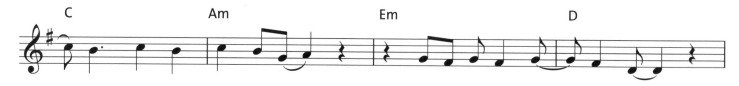

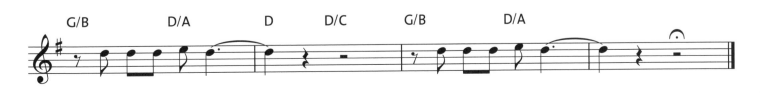

Apologize

Words & Music by Ryan Tedder
© Copyright 2005 Sony/ATV Tunes LLC/
Write 2 Live Publishing/Velvet Hammer Music, USA.
Sony/ATV Music Publishing.
All Rights Reserved. International Copyright Secured.

Soulfully ♩ = 118

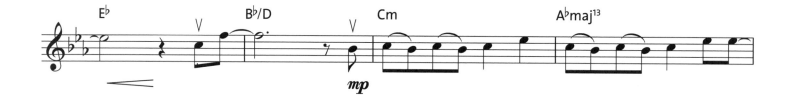

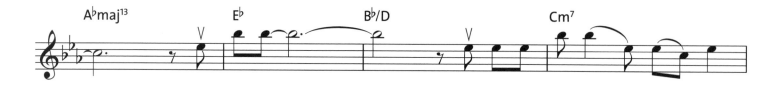

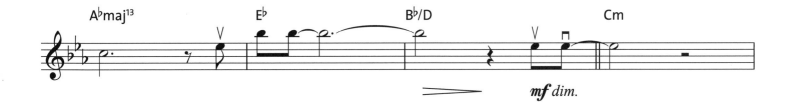

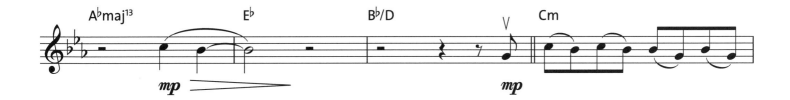

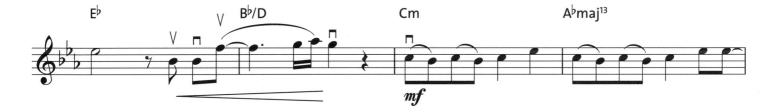

Brown Eyed Girl

Words & Music by Van Morrison
© Copyright 1967 Web IV Music Incorporated, USA.
Universal Music Publishing Limited.
All rights in Germany administered by Universal Music Publ. GmbH.
All Rights Reserved. International Copyright Secured.

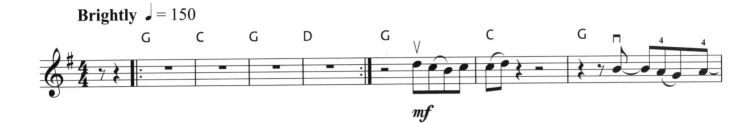

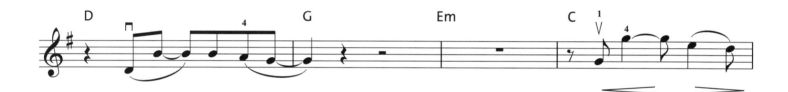

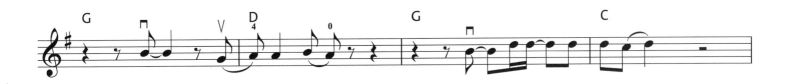

Repeat to fade

Can You Feel The Love Tonight (from Walt Disney Pictures' 'The Lion King')

Words by Tim Rice
Music by Elton John

Calmly ♩ = 63

poco rit.

6 *Chasing Pavements*

Words & Music by Adele Adkins & Eg White

Tenderly ♩ = 80

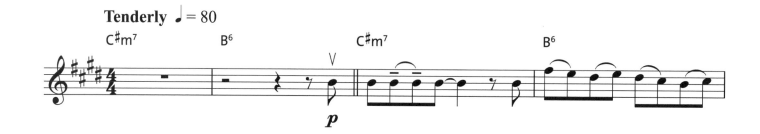

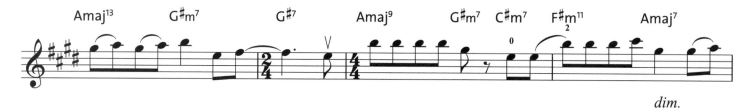

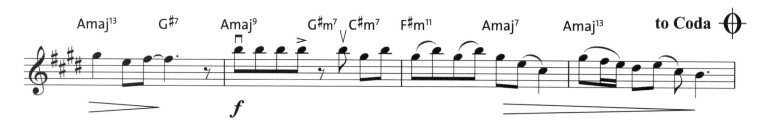

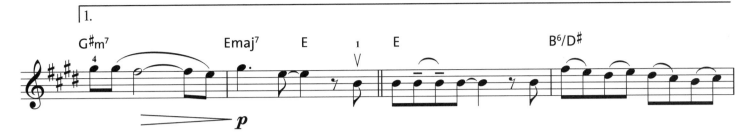

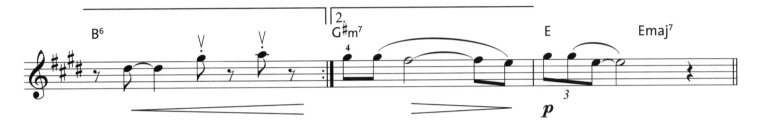

D.S. al Coda   ⊕ **Coda**

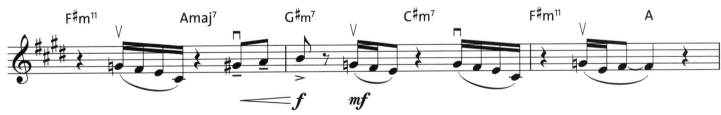

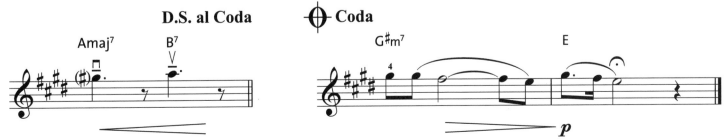

Dancing Queen

Words & Music by Benny Andersson,
Stig Anderson & Björn Ulvaeus

Moderate rock

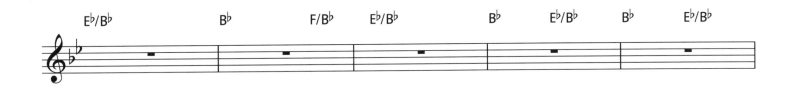

Repeat and fade

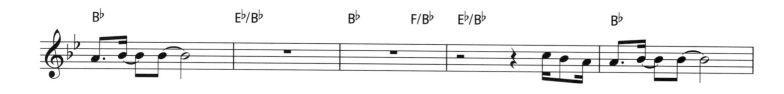

Hallelujah

Words & Music by Leonard Cohen

mf *cantabile*

f

mf *espressivo*

molto rall.

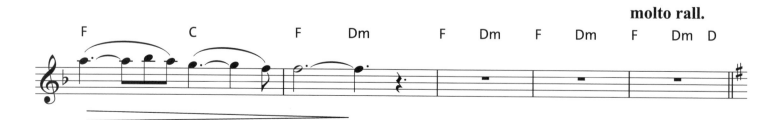

A tempo

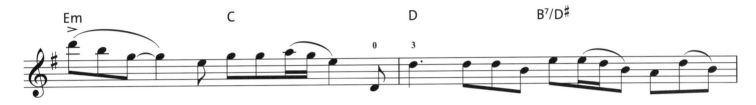

rit.

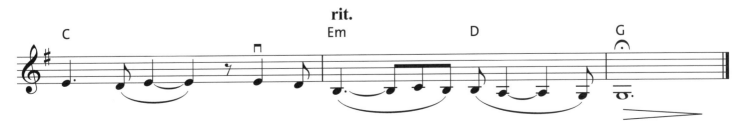

9 *If I Were A Boy*

Words & Music by Tobias Gad & Britney Carlson

Steadily and rhythmically ♩ = 90

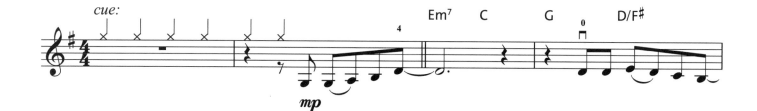

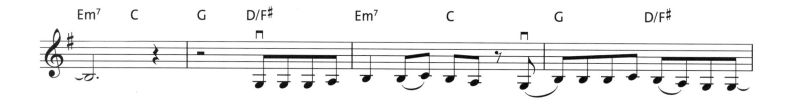

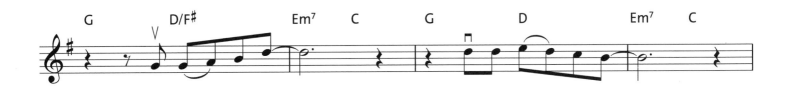

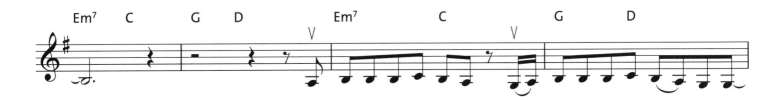

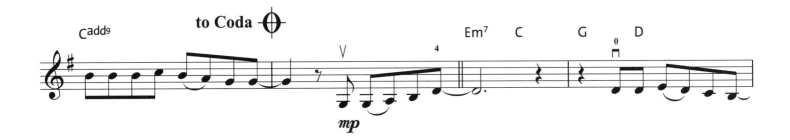

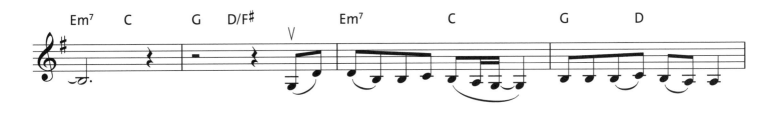

D.S. al Coda

Coda

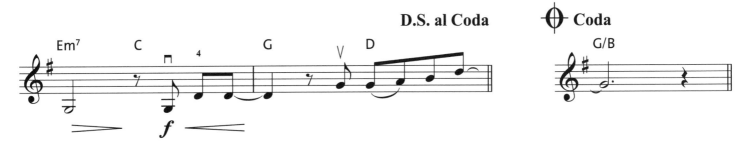

23

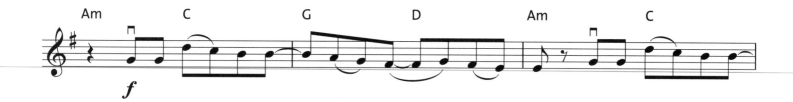

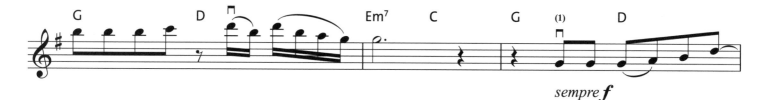

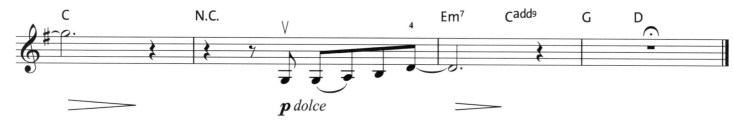

(I've Had) The Time Of My Life

Words & Music by Frankie Previte,
John DeNicola & Donald Markowitz

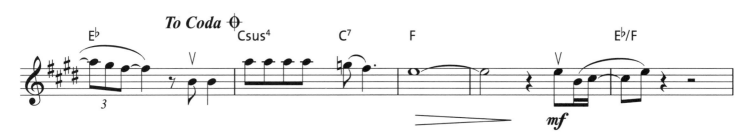

Man In The Mirror

Words & Music by Glen Ballard & Siedah Garrett

Steadily, with a bounce ♩ = 100

N.C.

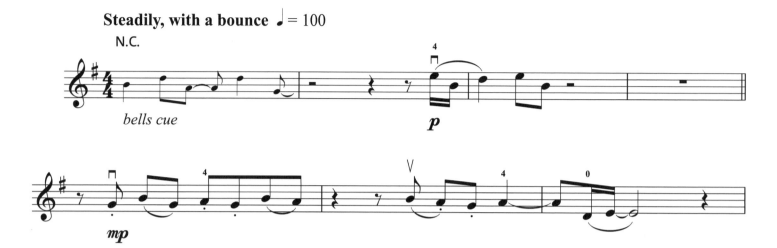

bells cue

p

mp

G   D/F#   Em⁷   D

Cadd9   G   D/F#   Em⁷

D   3   Cadd9

Am⁷   Gadd9/B   Cadd9

cresc. poco a poco

Gadd9/B   Am⁷   Gadd9/B   Cadd9

cresc.

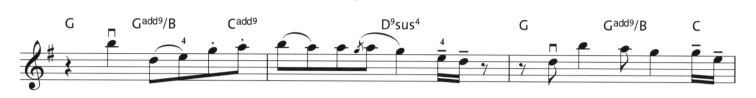

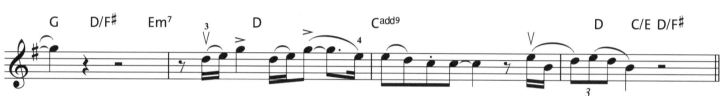

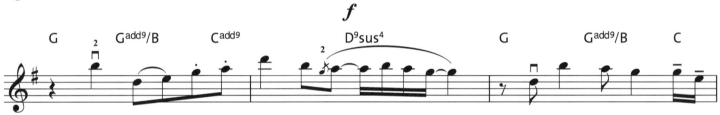

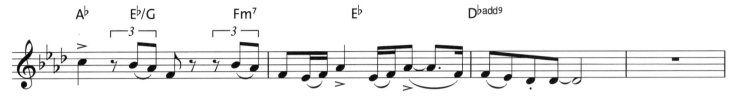

12 Ring Of Fire

Words & Music by Merle Kilgore & June Carter

© Copyright 1962 Painted Desert Music Corporation, USA.
Shapiro Bernstein & Company Limited.
All Rights Reserved. International Copyright Secured.

Upbeat Country ♩ = 104

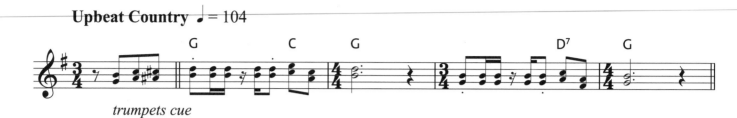

trumpets cue

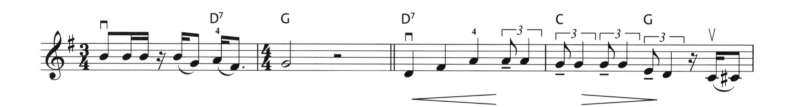

trumpets cue

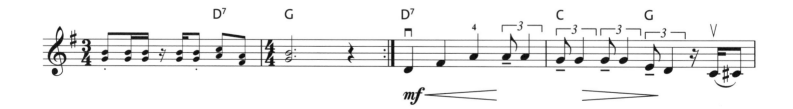

mf

trumpets cue

f

mp

Repeat to fade

dim. poco a poco

My Way

Words & Music by Claude Francois, Jacques Revaux & Gilles Thibaut

Straight quavers ♩ = 74

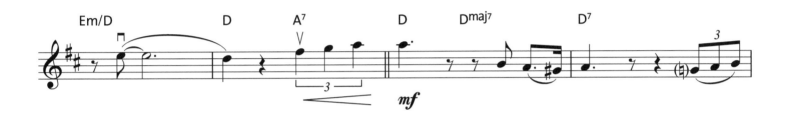

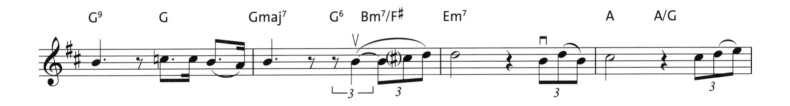

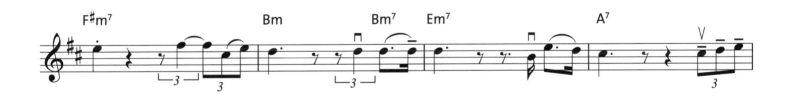

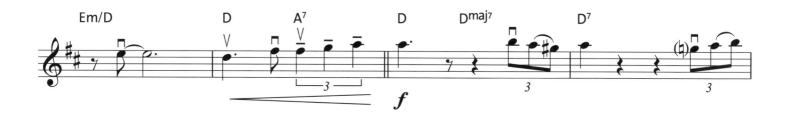

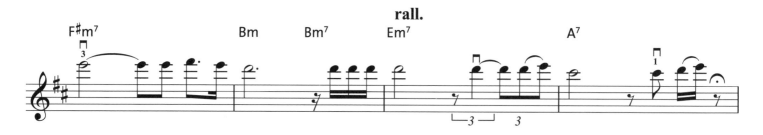

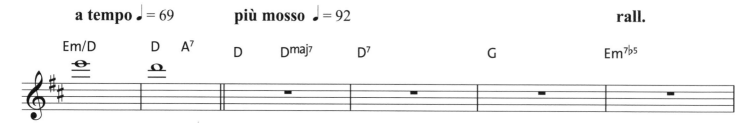

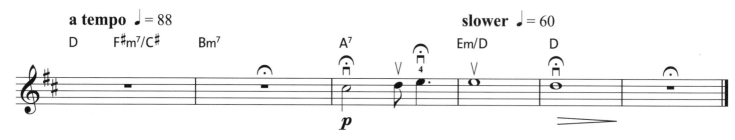

Stayin' Alive

Words & Music by Barry Gibb, Maurice Gibb & Robin Gibb

With a Disco groove ♩ = 104

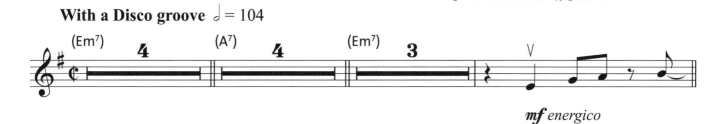

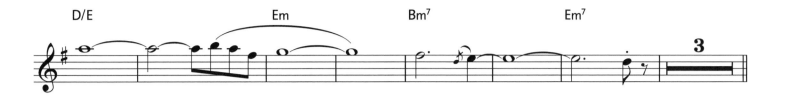

mp energico

mf

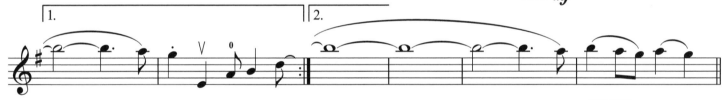

mf

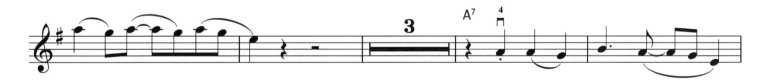

Repeat twice, to fade on 2nd repeat

f

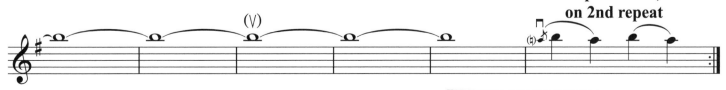

Take On Me

Words & Music by Morten Harket,
Mags Furuholmen & Pal Waaktaar

© Copyright 1984 ATV Music Limited.
Sony/ATV Music Publishing.
All Rights Reserved. International Copyright Secured.

Briskly ♩ = 170

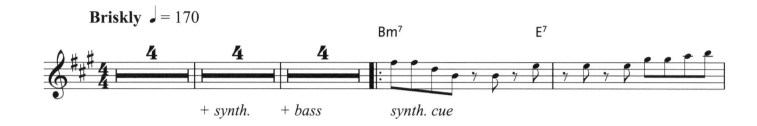

+ synth.   + bass   synth. cue

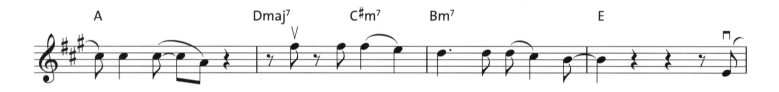

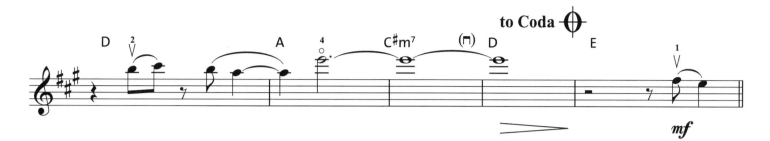

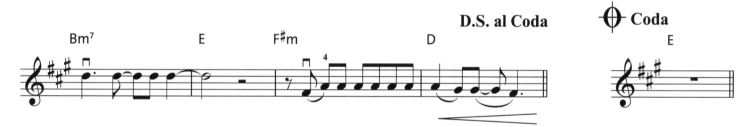

41

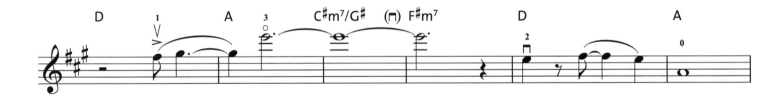

Fade to end

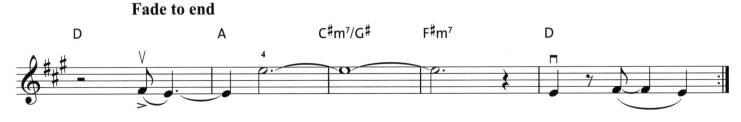

A Whiter Shade Of Pale

Words & Music by Matthew Fisher,
Keith Reid & Gary Brooker

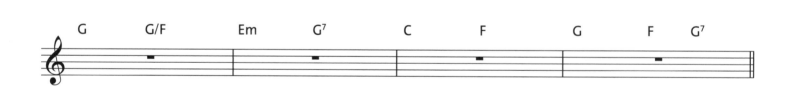

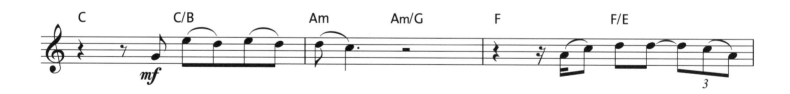

rall.

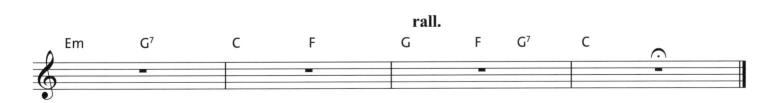

17 *Viva La Vida*

Words & Music by Guy Berryman, Jon Buckland,
Will Champion & Chris Martin
© Copyright 2008 Universal Music Publishing MGB Limited.
All rights in Germany administered by Musik Edition Discoton GmbH
(a division of Universal Music Publishing Group).
All Rights Reserved. International Copyright Secured.

Lightly ♩ = 138

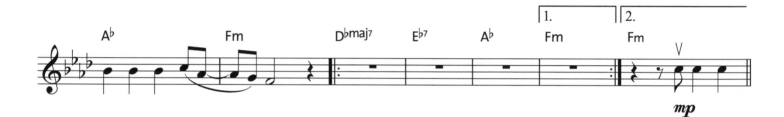

to Coda ⊕

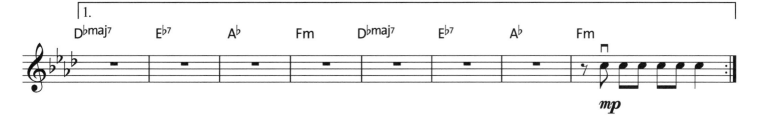

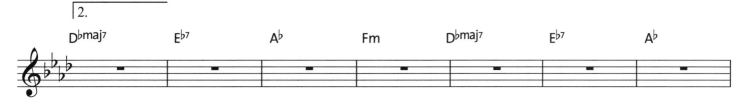

D.S. al Coda   ⊕ Coda

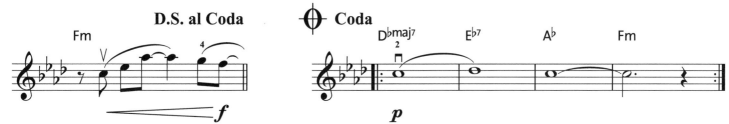

123456789

CD backing tracks

1. **TUNING NOTE**

2. **AMERICAN PIE**
(McLean) Universal/MCA Music Limited

3. **APOLOGIZE**
(Tedder) Sony/ATV Music Publishing (UK) Limited

4. **BROWN EYED GIRL**
(Morrison) Universal Music Publishing Limited

5. **CAN YOU FEEL THE LOVE TONIGHT**
(Rice/John) Warner/Chappell Artemis Music Limited

6. **CHASING PAVEMENTS**
(Adkins/Eg White) Universal Music Publishing Limited.

7. **DANCING QUEEN**
(Andersson/Anderson/Ulvaeus) Bocu Music Limited

8. **HALLELUJAH**
(Cohen) Sony/ATV Music Publishing (UK) Limited

9. **IF I WERE A BOY**
(Gad/Carlson) Cherry Lane Music Limited/Universal/MCA Music Limited

10. **(I'VE HAD) THE TIME OF MY LIFE**
(Previte/DeNicola/Markowitz) Worldsong Incorporated/Sony/ATV Music Publishing
(UK) Limited/EMI Music Publishing Limited/Songs Of Pen UK

11. **MAN IN THE MIRROR**
(Ballard/Garrett) Universal/MCA Music Limited/Cherry Lane Music Limited

12. **RING OF FIRE**
(Kilgore/Carter) Shapiro Bernstein & Company Limited.

13. **MY WAY**
(Francois/Revaux/Thibaut)
Warner/Chappell Overseas Holdings/Because Publishing Limited/Gilles Thibaut/
Jacques Revauz/Claude Francois

14. **STAYIN' ALIVE**
(B.Gibb/M.Gibb/R.Gibb)
Warner/Chappell Music Limited/Universal Music Publishing MGB

15. **TAKE ON ME**
(Harket/Furuholmen/Waaktaar) Sony/ATV Music Publishing (UK) Limited

16. **A WHITER SHADE OF PALE**
(Fisher/Reid/Brooker) Onward Music Limited.

17. **VIVA LA VIDA**
(Berryman/Buckland/Champion/Martin) Universal Music Publishing MGB Limited

How to use the CD

The tuning notes on track 1 are A, D, G and E, respectively.

After track 1, the backing tracks are listed in the order in
which they appear in the book. Look for the ⊙ symbol
in the book for the relevant backing track.